Miley Cyrus

by Leanne Currie-McGhee

LUCENT BOOKS

A part of Gale, Cengage Learning

GALE
CENGAGE Learning

Detroit • New York • San Francisco • New Haven, Conn • Waterville, Maine • London

GALE
CENGAGE Learning™

LIBRARY OF CONGRESS CATALOGING-IN-PUBLICATION DATA

Currie-McGhee, L. K. (Leanne K.)
   Miley Cyrus / By Leanne Currie-McGhee.
       p. cm. — (People in the news)
   Includes bibliographical references and index.
   ISBN 978-1-4205-0127-8 (hardcover)
   1. Cyrus, Miley, 1992—Juvenile literature. 2. Singers—United States—Biography—Juvenile literature. 3. Television actors and actresses—United States—Biography—Juvenile literature. I. Title.
   ML3930.C98C87 2009
   782.42164092—dc22
   [B]

                                                         2008050904

Lucent Books
27500 Drake Rd.
Farmington Hills, MI 48331

ISBN-13: 978-1-4205-0127-8
ISBN-10: 1-4205-0127-5

Printed in the United States of America
1 2 3 4 5 6 7 13 12 11 10 09

Contents

F ame and celebrity are alluring. People are drawn to those who walk in fame's spotlight, whether they are known for great accomplishments or for notorious deeds. The lives of the famous pique public interest and attract attention, perhaps because their experiences seem in some ways so different from, yet in other ways so similar to, our own.

Newspapers, magazines, and television regularly capitalize on this fascination with celebrity by running profiles of famous people. For example, television programs such as *Entertainment Tonight* devote all of their programming to stories about entertainment and entertainers. Magazines such as *People* fill their pages with stories of the private lives of famous people. Even newspapers, newsmagazines, and television news frequently delve into the lives of well-known personalities. Despite the number of articles and programs, few provide more than a superficial glimpse at their subjects.

Lucent's People in the News series offers young readers a deeper look into the lives of today's newsmakers, the influences that have shaped them, and the impact they have had in their fields of endeavor and on other people's lives. The subjects of the series hail from many disciplines and walks of life. They include authors, musicians, athletes, political leaders, entertainers, entrepreneurs, and others who have made a mark on modern life and who, in many cases, will continue to do so for years to come.

These biographies are more than factual chronicles. Each book emphasizes the contributions, accomplishments, or deeds that have brought fame or notoriety to the individual and shows how that person has influenced modern life. Authors portray their subjects in a realistic, unsentimental light. For example, Bill Gates—the cofounder and chief executive officer of the software giant Microsoft—has been instrumental in making personal computers the most vital tool of the modern age. Few dispute his business savvy, his perseverance, or his technical expertise, yet critics say he is ruthless in his dealings with competitors and driven more by his desire to maintain Microsoft's dominance in the computer industry than by an interest in furthering technology.

In these books, young readers will encounter inspiring stories about real people who achieved success despite enormous obstacles. Oprah Winfrey—the most powerful, most watched, and wealthiest woman on television today—spent the first six years of her life in the care of her grandparents while her unwed mother sought work and a better life elsewhere. Her adolescence was colored by promiscuity, pregnancy at age fourteen, rape, and sexual abuse.

Each author documents and supports his or her work with an array of primary and secondary source quotations taken from diaries, letters, speeches, and interviews. All quotes are footnoted to show readers exactly how and where biographers derive their information and provide guidance for further research. The quotations enliven the text by giving readers eyewitness views of the life and accomplishments of each person covered in the People in the News series.

In addition, each book in the series includes photographs, annotated bibliographies, timelines, and comprehensive indexes. For both the casual reader and the student researcher, the People in the News series offers insight into the lives of today's newsmakers—people who shape the way we live, work, and play in the modern age.

Miley at Madame Tussauds

Miley Cyrus knew that she had truly made it when Madame Tussauds Wax Museum made a wax figure of her. In March 2008, at just fifteen years old, Miley Cyrus was immortalized in wax at New York's Madame Tussauds.

Miley is one of the most famous teenagers in the world. She plays Hannah Montana on Disney's *Hannah Montana* show. Millions of teenagers and preteens have become fans of the show, its music, and Miley Cyrus.

Hannah Montana Rises to Fame

On the show, Miley plays Miley Stewart, a normal girl by day, who has a secret. She is also a famous pop star, Hannah Montana, but no one except her family and close friends knows. Miley Cyrus does both the singing and acting as her character. She plays alongside a cast that includes her father, country singer Billy Ray Cyrus, who plays her father on the show.

Since its inception, *Hannah Montana* has become the number one cable series for kids aged six to fourteen. The show has become so popular that it has led to soundtracks, DVDs, and movies. It has even led to Hannah Montana merchandise. According to *People* magazine, Hannah Montana merchandise, including bedding, toys, clothes, and more, is expected to bring in $1 billion to Disney for the fiscal year 2007–2008.

Miley's take of all of this merchandise has made her a very wealthy young woman. In addition to getting a percentage of the

Fans surround the wax figure of Miley Cyrus at Madame Tussauds Wax Museum in New York City's Times Square in March 2008.

merchandise sales, she makes millions from her *Hannah Montana* show, soundtracks, and movies. She took home $17.5 million for her concert tour as Hannah Montana.

Rock Star, Too

Miley's fame continued to grow. She became a pop star when the songs she sang as Hannah Montana were released on Radio Disney. The show's fans began to tune in to the radio to hear Miley

Fans of singer Miley Cyrus admire the Hannah Montana clothing and accessories display at the Licensing International Expo in New York City in June 2007.

sing. Disney took these songs and released them on a soundtrack from the show. The soundtrack was an immediate success. This soundtrack sold 3.5 million copies in the United States.

Miley's fans bought and loved the soundtrack. Disney decided to see if Miley's fans would also like songs Miley had cowritten. On the second soundtrack from *Hannah Montana*, half of the soundtrack includes Hannah Montana songs written by other artists that Miley performs. The other half of the soundtrack includes songs both cowritten and sung by Miley. This album was also a big success and sold 3 million copies.

Concert Tour

Miley's popularity led to a major concert tour. In 2007 she began a sixty-nine-date *Best of Both Worlds* concert tour. During the first half of each performance she dressed up as Hannah Montana and performed Hannah Montana songs. After the first half, Miley would go backstage, take off her Hannah Montana outfit and makeup, and come back onstage dressed as herself. Miley would then sing her own songs that she cowrote. Tickets sold out within minutes. Miley filled twenty-thousand-seat stadiums with ease. Parents desperate to get tickets for the concert were willing to pay as high as $2,500 for a single ticket.

Some parents even lied trying to get tickets. A six-year-old girl wrote an essay that won her four tickets to a sold-out Hannah Montana concert. She wrote the essay about how her father had died while serving in Iraq. The essay turned out to be a complete lie. Her mom, Priscilla Ceballos, admitted that she and her daughter deliberately lied on the essay so they could win the contest.

Fortunately fans who could not get to the concerts had the opportunity to see Miley sing on the big screen. Disney realeased the *Best of Both Worlds Concert 3D* movie, which chronicled her tour. The movie grossed more than $60 million.

Dealing with Fame

Miley's success has had some downsides. At a young age, she has dealt with the more difficult aspects of being a celebrity. For example,

Miley Cyrus performs at a concert in Irvine, California, on May 10, 2008.

whenever she goes out, Miley is constantly followed by reporters and photographers. Because of this, she has no private life. Nearly everything she does or says is recorded and scrutinized.

Miley, her parents, and four brothers and sisters even had to move because of her fame. They left their old house in California because they needed one with a gated entrance. Before they moved, every day young Hannah Montana fans rang the Cyrus doorbell wanting to meet Miley.

Miley feels she can handle the more difficult aspects of her fame. She says that her close family and faith keep her grounded. Her parents are determined to keep her from becoming another teen star who ends up in the tabloids because of excessive partying. "People will say, 'Well, you're only 14. You're not getting the same pressures as [stars like Britney Spears],'" she says. "It's like . . . 'Yes, I am.' It's because, you know, this life that I lead is pretty crazy. It's just about, you know, having value and having pride in yourself."[1]

What's Next?

Miley has no plans to take a break. She wants to keep growing in her career. In 2008 she worked on *Breakout*. Unlike her other alubms, there will be no Hannah Montana songs that are written by other artists. Instead, *Breakout* will consist entirely of songs both cowritten and sung by Miley. The album debuted at number one in July 2008.

For all that she has accomplished, Miley's career is really just starting. As she says, "Hopefully I can continue working on music, acting, whatever comes along. After the movie, I'll start working on some other cool thing."[2] Whatever the next cool thing is, if Miley's fans remain true to her, it will be a success.

Chapter 1

Named for Greatness

From when she was a toddler, Miley Cyrus knew she wanted to become a performer. Throughout her early childhood and elementary school, she developed the drive to achieve this dream. Her parents raised her to believe she could accomplish this dream as long as she focused on using her talents to give back to the world.

Miley was born in Franklin, Tennessee, on November 23, 1992, to Billy Ray and Leticia "Tish" Finley Cyrus. To them Miley symbolized the beginning of a new part of their lives. Miley was the first child they had together. Billy Ray had a son, Christopher Cody, with girlfriend Kristen Luckey, not long before Miley was born. Tish had daughter Brandi and son Trace with her first husband.

Billy Ray and Tish named their daughter Destiny Hope Cyrus—later she was nicknamed Miley. Miley's parents chose her name because they believed she would accomplish great things in life. "She was named [Destiny Hope] because her mother and I always felt . . . before she was born that [her] destiny was to bring hope to the world,"[3] says Billy Ray.

Miley's parents thought there was a good chance she would grow up to be a talented girl. They believed she would inherit her father's musical talents. Her father, Billy Ray Cyrus, is a successful country singer. He released his debut album, *Some Gave All*, in 1992, the same year Miley was born. The album sold over 9 million copies. *Some Gave All* debuted at the top of both the Top

Country singer Billy Ray Cyrus holds his nearly two-year-old daughter Miley at an Elvis Presley tribute concert in Memphis, Tennessee, in October 1994.

Country Albums and Billboard 200. On both charts it stayed at the top for thirty-four and seventeen weeks, respectively. Cyrus's most famous hit from the album was the single "Achy Breaky Heart." This song made him $40 million. The same year he was nominated for five Grammy Awards.

Brings the Family Together

Billy Ray Cyrus was at the top of his fame and making lots of money the year before Miley was born. However, he was not happy in his personal life. He and Cindy Smith, whom he met before he became famous, married in 1986 and divorced in 1991. After the divorce, Cyrus partied and dated different women in the months immediately following the divorce.

He met and fell in love with Tish in 1991 but still did not settle down. He continued touring and partying on the road. In 1992 Tish discovered she was pregnant with Billy Ray's baby. Tish's pregnancy with Miley changed the course of Billy Ray's life.

Cyrus realized that he had a choice to make. "I was either going to be responsible, or I wasn't," he said. "Am I gonna be a dad, or I'm not. Am I gonna be a husband, or I'm not. Are we going to be a family, or we're not. It's that 'not' thing that made me feel very sad and lonely."[4]

Cyrus made a decision to change his focus from his career and life on the road to making a family with Tish. "You know what, this train may come off the tracks, but I'm going to be a dad," he said. "I'm going to be a husband, and try to have something in my life that is right."[5] He married Tish and decided to devote himself to his family.

As Normal as Possible

After he and Tish married, Billy Ray wanted to give his family as normal a life as possible. He decided to step out of the limelight. Although he continued writing songs, he decided to stop going on extended tours and instead stay home with his family. He and Tish bought Singing Hills, a 500-acre (202-ha) property outside Nashville, Tennessee, and settled there.

The Cyrus family filled the house. Billy Ray, Tish, Miley, Brandi, and Trace all moved into their new home. Billy Ray even adopted Brandi and Trace because he wanted to be their legal father. Although Christopher, Billy Ray's son with his former girlfriend, lived with his mother, he regularly visited his father at the Cyrus home. After Miley's birth, Billy Ray and Tish went on to have son Braison and daughter Noah.

Disney Channel superstar Miley Cyrus at the premiere of High School Musical 2 with (left to right) her father Billy Ray, mother Tish, sister Noah, and brother Braison.

As Miley was growing up, her parents stressed the importance of family togetherness. Her father enjoyed teaching them fun activities. "I taught [my kids] how to build a good snowman, how to ride a motorcycle, how to ride a horse, how to roast a wiener properly over a fire, and a good marshmallow," says Billy Ray. "You know, those type of things, I was good at that."[6]

Miley and her brothers and sisters also had fun by playing silly pranks on one another. Her brother Braison remembers hiding a wooden snake in Miley's bed. She screamed and chased after him, thinking it was real. In addition to pranks and fun, like most brothers and sisters, Miley and her siblings fought with one another. "I'm the middle child, so I've got an older brother and sister who will be like, 'You're acting so immature' and then I'll say, 'Well, I am younger than you!'" Miley explains. "Then I've got a younger brother and sister and I'll say that to them, and they'll say the same thing back."[7]

In addition to being surrounded by kids, Miley has always had a lot of animals. Being on a farm, she was able to have more pets

Smiley Miley

Destiny Hope Cyrus became Miley early in her life. Her nickname, Miley, is the result of being a happy baby. "As a baby, she always smiled," her dad, Billy Ray Cyrus, remembers. Because of this, her family always called her Smiley. Eventually, Smiley was shortened into Miley. "Smiley evolved into Miley in baby slang," Billy Ray explains. Soon her family and friends called her Miley all the time. The nickname stuck and became the name that everyone used for Destiny Hope. Today only her grandmother continues to call her Destiny. Miley even decided to change her name legally. In 2008, with the support of her parents, she officially became Miley Ray Cyrus.

Quoted in Lorrie Lynch, "Who's News?" *USA Weekend*, February 24, 2008. www.usaweekend.com/08_issues/080224/080224whosnews-celebs-birthdays.html#cyrus.

than most kids. "I have lots of pets," she says. "I have eight horses, six dogs, a fish, two cats and chickens. I used to have a rat, but he died. I think that's it. When I'm older I want my house to be a total zoo because I love animals."[8]

Faith First

Throughout her childhood, Miley's parents instilled in Miley and her siblings the importance of faith in God. Religion was an essential part of Billy Ray and Tish's lives. They are both devout Christians.

Billy Ray and Tish stressed that whatever the children did, it should be for God, because any of their talents were gifts from God. Billy Ray felt this way about his own musical talents. As he explains, "I know all things that are good come from Almighty God above. I count my blessings every single day. Every day I pray God will show me the doors He wants me to walk through, the people He wants me to talk to, the songs He wants me to sing. I want to be the light He wants me to be in this world."[9]

To ground their children in the Christian faith, Billy Ray and Tish attended a Christian church regularly. Sundays were always a time for the family to be together and worship God. Additionally they included prayer as a daily part of their lives.

Following Her Father's Footsteps

Miley enjoyed a normal life that included church, school, friends, and hobbies. In addition to this, she spent much of her time watching her father at work. This made Miley realize she wanted to be an entertainer like him. Even though he no longer traveled on major tours, Billy Ray continued to work as a musician. He recorded and released *It Won't Be the Last* in 1993, *Storm in the Heartland* in 1994, *Trail of Tears* in 1996, *Shot Full of Love* in 1998, and *Southern Rain* in 2000. He experimented with different types of music, not just country, and recorded some rock and blues songs.

Miley often accompanied Billy Ray when he recorded these albums. She also attended the few concerts he still did and loved watching him perform. Miley realized she wanted to be on the stage like her father. She dreamed of singing for audiences.

After the birth of Miley Cyrus, her father, Billy Ray Cyrus, stopped traveling on major tours. He continued recording and performing at small venues, such as at Dollywood, in Pigeon Forge, Tennessee, shown here in April 1993.

Acting Bug

Miley also discovered that she wanted to act. This was due to Billy Ray's interest in acting. In 1999 Miley's father decided that he wanted to become an actor in addition to a singer. He managed to get some small roles in different movies. He had a small role in famous director David Lynch's film *Mulholland Drive*.

After a few years, Billy Ray became dissatisfied with his choice of acting roles. As a Christian, he wanted to act in films with morals. He wanted to set an example for all people, particularly his children. Right around this time, the producers of the series *Doc* contacted Billy Ray. They told him that they wanted him for the title role. After reading the pilot episode, Billy Ray realized that his prayer to find an inspiring role had been answered.

Billy Ray landed the role of a country doctor on *Doc*, shown on PAX, a Christian cable TV network. Billy Ray was drawn to the show because it was family-friendly and based on values. *Doc* was a Christian-themed drama about a small-town doctor in New York City. It was an immediate hit for PAX with over 3.1 million viewers.

With its success, Billy Ray had a steady acting job in Toronto, Canada, where the show was filmed. During *Doc*'s four seasons, the entire Cyrus family spent most of their time in Canada to be with Billy Ray. While in Canada, Miley and her brothers and sisters were able to visit Billy Ray's set and watch him work.

After watching *Doc*'s filming, Miley knew that she also wanted to act. According to Miley, she discovered she liked acting "by going

Billy Ray Cyrus and co-star Andrea Robinson joke around on the set of the Doc television series.

to the set with my dad and getting to see the environment and how much fun, joy, and encouragement there is on the set. It's great seeing everyone working together as a team on the show. You are all together and you're all a family and it's a really great place to be."[10]

Improving Her Skills

Miley realized that if she wanted to be a musician and actress, she needed to practice. She used most of her free time to sing and act. According to Miley's mother, "from the time she was two and three years old, she would stand at Billy Ray's dad's house on the stairs and sing 'Tomorrow' at the top of her lungs."[11] Miley also always sang in the shower, sometimes staying in there forty-five minutes as she gave her own concert.

As she got older, Miley actively sought ways to improve her abilities. Her father taught her to play guitar. She practiced with him often. For them, it was both a way to improve their skills and to bond together. "Since Miley was a little girl, we've been writing songs together," her father said. "We sing together. We do a whole lot more of it offstage than onstage. That's how we really communicate the best with each other."[12]

Runs in the Family

Miley Cyrus is not the only one of her siblings who developed the dream to perform. Her younger sister, Noah Cyrus, born in 2000, is also determined to be an actress. Not yet ten years old, she has already had smaller roles in many projects. As a toddler, she had a small recurring role in *Doc*. Recently she played a small role on *Hannah Montana*. Miley's older sister, Brandi, also acts and has appeared in *Zoey 101*. Miley's older brother Trace is a vocalist and plays guitar in the rock band Metro Station, which has a recording contract. He started the band with Mason Musso, brother of Mitchel Musso, who is on the show *Hannah Montana*.

Miley decided she needed to do even more to improve her skills. She got involved in acting and singing at her school, Heritage Elementary School. One of her teachers, Nancy Sevier, remembers how Miley performed as a child. "You knew she was going to do something in music," Sevier said. "It never bothered her to be talking in front of the group. She was in total command of an audience."[13]

Miley also decided to take acting and singing lessons. "I started with a coach . . . in Toronto," Miley says. "I took singing and acting classes to make myself better because I really wanted to take it seriously and I didn't want people to think that I was just getting a break because of my dad."[14]

Parental Concerns

Initially Miley's parents did not want her to enter the entertainment field at such a young age. Although they knew she was talented, they also knew the difficulties of a performer's life. Specifically Billy Ray did not want Miley to have to endure the rejections that come along with being an aspiring actor or singer.

Billy Ray tried to persuade her not to get into acting. He did not want her to have to deal with rejection. "I'd see those little tears come down her face and I'd hold her and say, 'Enjoy being a kid. There is too much heartache to mess up your childhood,'" Billy Ray says of the times Miley would get rejected for a part. "She kept stepping up to the plate, and danggone, the right opportunity came at the right time."[15]

Tish was also concerned about Miley starting a career so young. Her main concern was that Miley would not get to enjoy being a kid if she became an actress. "I told Miley . . . you better hold off to do this," Tish stated. "Stay in school, go to prom . . . but that's not what she wanted."[16] Although she and Billy Ray had concerns, they could see that Miley was determined. Miley's parents decided to become her agents and actively pursue opportunities to build a career.

Lucky Breaks

With her parents' help in finding opportunities, Miley started to get some jobs in the music business. For example, she got a job

in a video. Miley appeared in bluegrass musician Rhonda Vincent's music video for "If Heartaches Have Wings."

When Miley was twelve her dad helped her become a spokesperson for Daisy Rock Guitars. Daisy Rock is the world's first and only company that supplies and markets guitars for females. Daisy guitars have a slim neck profile, which makes it easier for women and girls, who typically have smaller hands then men, to play guitar. Additionally the guitars are lightweight, so a person with a small build can play them easier than a typical guitar. "Miley Cyrus personifies the mission of Daisy Rock to empower girls and young people to play music and reach their goals!"[17] said Daisy Rock President Tish Ciravolo. Miley received an Acoustic Electric Pink Sparkle guitar on June 13, 2004, at the Country Music Association Music Festival in Nashville, Tennessee. After receiving the guitar, she became one of Daisy Rock's youngest endorsees ever.

Miley also got to sing in a show because of her father. In 2004 Miley sang on the twenty-second annual Colgate Country Showdown with her dad, who was the host and a former contestant of the annual show. Colgate Country Showdown is a talent search for country singers and begins each spring with over 450

Daisy Rock Guitar founder and president Tish Ciravolo poses with one of the company's guitars. At the age of twelve, Miley Cyrus became a spokesperson for the manufacturer of guitars for females.

local talent contests sponsored by country music radio stations throughout the United States. After going through state and regional contests, winners get to the National Final, which is televised to a national audience. During the show, Miley came out with her father, and together they sang "Holding On to a Dream," a song from Billy Ray's album.

Acting Career Takes Off

Miley's father also helped her get acting parts. She played extras in her father's films. Then she landed a small role in *Doc* and worked alongside her father. Miley played the character Kiley for three episodes on the show.

In 2003 Miley landed a role in director Tim Burton's movie *Big Fish*. Several famous actresses and actors, including Ewan McGregor, Billy Crudup, Steve Buscemi, and Jessica Lange, appeared in the movie. Miley got the part of Young Ruthie and was credited as Destiny Cyrus.

Following these successes Miley began to get some press. She was featured in magazine articles in *Parade* and *Country Weekly*. Becoming known in her own right gave Miley the confidence to try for even bigger roles. Soon her confidence and hard work would pay off in a big way.

Chapter 2

Big Break

By the time Miley was eleven, her parents' perseverance in finding potential acting jobs for her, as well as her own hard work when auditioning for roles, resulted in Miley getting several small parts in shows and movies. After landing a role in *Big Fish*, she became more well known as a child actor. She hoped this would lead to bigger roles in other projects.

Miley's hope came true when she and her parents learned about an opportunity at Disney Studios. To get on a Disney show is a major accomplishment for a young actor or actress. Disney is often able to turn its preteen and teenage actors and actresses into stars. For this reason, Miley really wanted the Disney part. She decided to do all she could to get it.

The Disney Formula

The reason a Disney role is so coveted is that Disney has developed a winning formula for making popular preteen and teenage shows. In 2001 the Disney Channel began to create shows that were aimed at preteens, primarily eight- to twelve-year-olds.

Disney shows include pop music. Disney discovered that music draws in more viewers to the shows. Also, Disney realized that music could lead to other profitable ventures. Fans would not only watch the shows, but also buy the soundtracks from the shows and attend concerts featuring music from the shows.

One of the first shows of this kind was *Lizzie McGuire*, which starred Hilary Duff, who has since become a famous pop star and

The success of Hilary Duff and her television show Lizzie McGuire led Disney to want to continue the successful formula. That led to the creation of Hannah Montana.

actress. Disney released a *Lizzie McGuire* soundtrack that included songs used in the background of and inspired by the show. The soundtrack included a song by Duff. This led to Duff's own albums, some produced by Disney's Hollywood Records, which became popular and made Duff a pop star.

Disney's success with *Lizzie McGuire* inspired the company to continue following the formula. Next Disney created *The Cheetah Girls*, a music-based TV movie about four friends aspiring to be pop stars. The Cheetah Girls went on to perform in successful tours of the music from the movie and soundtrack. Disney combined acting and music in TV series such as *That's So Raven*, starring Raven-Symone. Raven sings on her series soundtrack. In January 2006 Disney released a TV movie, *High School Musical*, about high school kids trying out for a musical. The film received an Emmy Award, and the soundtrack was the best-selling album in the United States for 2006.

The show that interested Miley was called *Hannah Montana*. The premise of the show was an ordinary person in an extraordinary situation. The show's feature role was a teen girl leading a double life as a pop star and a regular student. The creators felt that kids would be able to relate to the girl's regular life and also get to experience, through the show, the pop star life. Disney executives were confident this show would be a hit. "Disney has become a hit machine and all cylinders are clicking," says Jason Maltby, president of New York–based MediaShare, an ad buying firm. "Its successes breed more successes and provide a platform for new shows like *Hannah Montana*."[18] To make the show a success, however, Disney needed to find a young star who could carry the show as an actress and a singer.

The Search Begins

In 2004 the search for the right actress to play Hannah Montana began. The search took nearly a year. Disney placed ads in acting publications such as *Back Stage West*. The ads invited young actresses to try out for the part of Chloe Stewart, the original name for Hannah Montana's alter ego. The following ad, from *Back Stage West*, ran in November 2004:

London Stroud Casting is accepting submissions for *Hannah Montana*, a half-hour sitcom pilot. Exec. prod/wrt. Michael Poryes. Shoot starts Jan. 10, 2005. Chloe Stewart: girl, Caucasian or Latina, 13–17, must be very good with comedy, to play pop star "Hannah Montana," really wants to fit in at school and is disguised as an everyday girl, must sing very well, series regular.[19]

Disney Channel executives wanted the lead actress to appeal to preteens and also to parents. Producers also wanted to find a young actress who was experienced enough to balance regular life with the demands of a TV show. They did not want a star who would end up in the tabloids partying or acting inappropriately. Additionally the lead actress had to have musical talent. "It takes patience," says Disney Channel Worldwide President Rich Ross of the search. "We needed someone with talent but also the maturity to handle the pressure."[20]

Miley heard of *Hannah Montana* and immediately sent in an audition tape. She sang Joan Jett's *I Love Rock 'n' Roll*. Initially she auditioned for the role of Lilly, the sidekick of the main character. Disney's talent scouts were impressed enough with Miley's tape to ask her to audition for the lead role.

Producers asked Miley to fly in for a face-to-face audition. Miley flew from Tennessee to California but did not get the role. She was eleven and seemed too small and young to carry a show, thought Gary Marsh, Disney Channel entertainment president. "She was completely green and had no professional experience and had never been the star of anything, let alone a real series."[21]

Miley's Persistence

The Disney Channel continued its search for another six months. Executives would not go forward until they were sure they had found just the right girl. They auditioned over a thousand girls in both New York and California. Marsh did not forget about Miley, however. She continued to send him audition tapes of herself.

Miley's persistence paid off. When she was twelve, Marsh called Miley in for another audition. Miley sang in front of Marsh and

*Miley Cyrus performs as Hannah Montana on ABC's Good
Morning America, June 22, 2007.*

Accent or Not?

Many movies and TV show producers prefer to hire actors who do not have accents. Growing up in Tennessee, Miley developed a strong Southern accent. Because she wanted to be an actress, Miley spent years working with voice and acting coaches to get rid of her Southern accent. When Disney executives finally chose her for the part of Hannah Montana, they surprised her with a request. "After I was selected, they said, 'Where's your accent? We want it back,'" Miley explains. She then had to work to get her accent back. "I had to go home for two weeks to regain it," she says. "I sometimes complain, 'I don't want to say it Southern.' They say, 'Say it Southern!'"

Quoted in David Hiltbrand, "Newfound Fame on Disney Shouldn't Faze Miley Cyrus," *Philadelphia Inquirer,* May 17, 2006.

fifteen other Disney professionals. Miley gave everything she could in the performance, just like every time she auditioned. "The process was basically repetitive, having to get up in front of people you've never met before and sing your heart out,"[22] Miley says.

"She walked into a conference room full of executives. She stood in front of us and knocked us out," he says. "I remember I came back to my desk that night and wrote a note to my team saying, 'This is either something extraordinary or a chance that didn't pay off.'"[23] Marsh decided to take the chance. Miley got the lead role in *Hannah Montana*.

Dad Gets a Break, Too

During the auditions for *Hannah Montana*, Billy Ray Cyrus also got a call from Disney. They wanted to know if he was interested in playing the part of the lead role's father. Billy Ray held off on auditioning until Disney cast the lead role for *Hannah Montana*. He did not want to be an influence on whether or not Miley got the part.

Billy Ray Cyrus and Miley Cyrus take a break on location during filming of Hannah Montana: The Movie *in July 2008.*

When Miley got the job as Hannah, Billy Ray decided he would be interested in working on the show if the part was still available. Disney had already chosen other actors to try out for the part. Since Billy Ray had previously said no, he was not on the list. Once Billy Ray expressed interest, the Disney Channel called him back. "[The Disney Channel] called and said, 'Hey, we're hiring the daddy tomorrow, but we'd like to take a meeting with you,'" Billy Ray remembers. "I went out there, and they kind of auditioned me, and, you know, it was just pretty obvious the chemistry between Miley and I is just so real."[24]

When Billy Ray auditioned, he did a scene with Miley. Miley had auditioned other men to play her father on the show, but the chemistry between her and her own father was immediately apparent. "They only made him audition once, the lucky duck," Miley says. "They were looking for father-daughter chemistry so it was pretty perfect."[25]

Miley was happy that her father was cast on the show. It made her feel safe and secure to know that he would be with her on the set. Also, the two of them had always been friends in addition to being father and daughter. She knew they would have fun together.

To California

The one downside of being on *Hannah Montana* was that the show taped in California. This meant Miley and her father had to move to California. The family always stuck together, so the entire Cyrus family left Tennessee.

Initially it took the family a while to get used to California. They missed their animals on the farm, their church, and their house. They had to leave their animals under their grandmother's care. When Miley first moved, she especially missed her favorite sport at school—cheerleading. "I'm not part of the school cheerleading squad in LA, because of work," says Miley. "But back in Nashville, I was on a professional team."[26] Miley had been active in competitive training with the Premier Tennessee All Stars. The team performed all over the country, winning various competitions.

Miley also left a lot of good friends in Tennessee and missed them when she arrived in California. However, her friends supported her move. They were not surprised that Disney picked her to play Hannah Montana. "Ever since I've known her," says Miley's best friend from Nashville, Lesley Patterson, "she's always been singing nonstop. My mom (Dolly Parton's personal assistant) used to tell her, 'Girl, you're going places.'"[27] Lesley and Miley continued to see each other during filming breaks and visits.

The California weather and great shopping soon won Miley over. A self-described shopaholic, she discovered the many stores in California. Miley admits that she particularly loves shoes and buys all different styles. She and her mom spent several afternoons together shopping for clothes and accessories.

The Show Begins

By the time Miley and her family moved to California, the Disney Channel was ready to film the first season of *Hannah Montana*. The creators and writers had spent much time writing a show that would appeal to both kids and adults. The creators were experienced in making shows like this. Michael Poryes, cocreator, also cocreated the Disney Channel's hit *That's So Raven*. Cocreator Rich Correll had over twenty years of TV experience creating family comedies, starting as an associate producer of *Happy Days*.

Once completed, the show resembled Miley's own life in some ways. *Hannah Montana* is about fourteen-year-old Miley Stewart, a girl from Tennessee, who moves to California to be a rock star. Miley Stewart leads a double life as an international singing sensation known as Hannah Montana by night and an ordinary girl during the day. Miley Stewart wears a blond wig and makeup whenever she appears as Hannah. On the show Miley lives with her widowed father, Robby, and her brother, Jackson. Robby, played by Miley's own father, is a former country singer, like Billy Ray himself.

This double life on the show is part of the fantasy that captures viewers. James Poniewozik of *Time* magazine writes:

Miley Cyrus appears at a Hollywood benefit with Hannah Montana costar Jason Earles, who plays her brother, in August 2006.

Hannah Montana is Superman for tween girls: she's got the secret identity, a more relevant superpower and a blond wig instead of a cape. But just as key to the show's success is her Clark Kent—the fictional Miley. Celebrity today is as rarefied as ever, yet with YouTube and reality TV, seems more accessible than ever. It's tantalizing but, as personified by Lindsay Lohan and Britney Spears, terrifying. Miley—a normal, grounded school kid—makes the fantasy safe. The theme song says it all: "You get the best of both worlds."[28]

Writers also felt that both kids and parents would be drawn to *Hannah Montana's* message. The message is that happiness comes when people follow their dreams but stay true to themselves. In the show, on-screen Miley is often tempted to reveal her alternate identity as Hannah Montana to her classmates in order to be popular. Ultimately Miley stays true to herself and lives her daily life without being a celebrity. "I think everybody has a goal or a dream, and just showing an average girl having her dream come true and still being able to balance her friends and her school is something they relate to," Miley says. "She's this big Hilary Duff–type celebrity, but that's as important on the show as her homework and her family and friends."[29]

Hannah Montana Music

A major part of *Hannah Montana* is the music. In many episodes, Hannah Montana sings and performs her songs. One of the main reasons that Miley got the part is her singing talent. Disney executives wanted the lead actress to have a strong voice.

Since music was such a major part of *Hannah Montana*, the producers and creators carefully chose its theme song. "Just Like You" and "The Other Side of Me," both of which are on the *Hannah Montana* soundtrack, were initially in the running for the theme song. However, *Hannah Montana* executives eventually decided that the theme song should be "The Best of Both Worlds."

"The Best of Both Worlds" is written by Matthew Gerrard and Robbie Nevil and is sung by Miley Cyrus. John Carta, who also

Name Changes

On *Hannah Montana*, Miley Cyrus plays Miley Stewart. However, that was not the character's original name. When first written, Miley Stewart was Zoe Stewart. Zoe Stewart was later changed to Chloe Stewart. Eventually Chloe Stewart became Miley Stewart after Miley Cyrus got the role. Lilly Truscott, Miley Stewart's best friend on the show, was originally named Lilly Romero. The name of Miley's alter ego, Hannah Montana, also changed a few times before Hannah was chosen. Three of the previous names were Anna Cabana, Samantha York, and Alexis Texas. Would Alexis Texas have been as popular as Hannah Montana? It is hard to know, but today fans cannot envision Hannah Montana by any other name.

composes the music cues for scene changes and commercial breaks in the show itself, composed the music for the song. The song's lyrics descibe Miley Stewart's double life as a pop star and regular student.

Matthew Gerrard and Robbie Nevil and several other writers wrote other songs sung by Hannah Montana on the show. Miley thinks that the songs are peppy and fun pop music. She describes Hannah Montana's music style as very similar to Kelly Clarkson, *American Idol* winner, whom Miley admires.

Life on the Set

Once Miley began work, most of her daily life was spent at Tribune Studios in Hollywood, where *Hannah Montana* is filmed. She immediately bonded with her costars Emily Osment and Mitchel Musso, both near her age. On the set they often joke around and play pranks. Mitchel says that Miley does the most pranks.

Off the set, Miley, Emily, and Mitchel also became friends. "Miley's been my best friend for the past three years. It's really easy-going on the set working with your best friends,"[30] Mitchel says of working together. He, Emily, and Miley text message each other on a regular basis. During filming, they go out for dinners and see movies together.

*The stars of Disney Channel's **Hannah Montana**: (left to right) Mitchel Musso, Billy Ray Cyrus, Miley Cyrus, Emily Osment, and Jason Earles.*

The three friends say that Disney promotes a family-friendly atmosphere on its shows. "Disney's been incredible," says Emily. "It's like one big family. We're always together, and no matter what we do, we just always have fun. That's just how Disney is, it's always big smiles and lots of laughter."[31]

At the end of the filming, Emily and Miley were sad to part for the break. "We cried because it was our last day of taping for season one," Miley says. "Emily was like, 'We live so close to each other, you're not gonna miss me.' Then I didn't see her for months! She was filming a movie and I was on tour."[32]

Miley also had fun working with her dad on the set. They have always been friends, joking with one another. They continued this relationship at work. "I get to do crazy stuff I wouldn't normally get away with, like pour Chinese food all over him. And when [he] got that load of cake in the face!" she explains. "I talk to the writers and make sure he gets hit with something at least twice a week."[33]

Miley does admit that working all day long with her father can be a bit too much. For example, she does not always love to drive to work with him. Miley complains about the music he likes to listen to.

Promoting the Premiere

When Miley finished filming the first season of *Hannah Montana*, she did not get a break. After filming, she needed to help Disney promote the show before it premiered. Miley interviewed with magazines, TV shows, and newspapers. She made appearances at publicity events. Meanwhile Disney also promoted the show with commercials on its radio and TV channels and through its own press kits to magazines and newspapers.

Additionally as part of the publicity for *Hannah Montana*, Disney executives decided to give a surprise Hannah Montana concert for a group of seven hundred kids. These kids, mainly preteens, were invited to see a concert and get the chance to be on TV. They were not told who would give the concert.

Miley had spent four days practicing with a coach and choreographer to get six songs right. She remembers being nervous about performing in front of people who had never heard of her.

"It was crazy because I was expecting dead silence," Miley says. "They had no idea who Hannah Montana was."[34] Despite this fact, the kids reacted with great enthusiasm at the concert. They screamed and cheered as though they were at a concert of a well-known pop star rather than someone they did not know. The enthusiastic reaction surprised Miley. She would soon discover that seven hundred cheering fans was just the beginning of her fame.

Chapter 3

Montana Mania

Disney executives were confident that *Hannah Montana* would be a hit and Miley Cyrus would become a star. The writers had developed a show that they believed preteens would find funny. They also believed parents would approve of the show's content. The musical composers had developed catchy songs. Additionally the show's cast was likable, and there was good chemistry on the set. Miley turned out to be a professional who was confident in both acting and singing. Lastly Disney ensured that people heard about the show, through commercials and interviews, before it even aired. Even so, the immediate sky-high popularity of *Hannah Montana* surprised them.

On Friday, March 24, 2006, at 9:30 P.M., the Disney Channel aired the first episode of *Hannah Montana*. The lead-in to the *Hannah Montana* debut was the premiere of an original movie, *Cow Belles*. *Cow Belles* drew 5.8 million viewers, which helped bring viewers to *Hannah Montana*. Additionally Corbin Bleu of *High School Musical*, the most-watched film in the history of the Disney Channel, guest starred on the first episode of *Hannah Montana* and brought in *High School Musical* fans. As a result the *Hannah Montana* series debut delivered 5.4 million total viewers.

Disney had never had a premiere that yielded 5.4 million viewers. Additionally the show beat out both broadcast and cable competition in its time period for kids aged nine to eleven. "This is an unbelievable response—beyond our wildest expectations," said Gary Marsh, president of entertainment at Disney Channel

Worldwide. "*Hannah Montana* has broken out like no other Disney Channel series ever."[35]

Who Is Watching?

The show immediately became popular with preteens. In its first year *Hannah Montana* averaged 3.5 million viewers during its Friday night showings. This made it the number one cable show among kids aged six to fourteen. During the same season, the show climbed to a number two rating against shows on at that time, not just cable channels, for that age group, second only to

Miley Cyrus greets fans at a Disney Channel event. Viewers aged six to fourteen are the target audience of Cyrus's hit TV show, Hannah Montana.

American Idol. By the second season the show was also appearing in 118 countries.

One of the reasons that kids like the show is that they can relate to character Miley's relationships to her friends and family. "I like how the writers just don't deal with superficial parent-and-teen issues," said Cheryl Hori, a high school junior who watches *Hannah Montana* every time she is home for an episode. "Miley and her dad butt heads. They have arguments. It feels more authentic."[36]

Another appealing aspect of the show is that normal kids can relate to Miley and her friends. Emily Osment, who plays Lilly on *Hannah Montana*, believes kids like the show because Miley and her friends are not part of the popular crowd. Emily explains:

> I think kids can connect with it a lot. Usually, on the Disney shows, the characters are usually really popular in school. In this show, it's sort of the opposite, because they're not so popular. Miley and Oliver, you know, they're not the most popular kids in school, and I think it gives kids something to relate to. It also gives the factor of *Hannah Montana*, which is every girl, or boy who wants to be a pop star. I wanted to be a pop star my entire life. Who doesn't want to be a pop star? It gives them those alter egos, and I think that's something that they can connect to and always want to be like.[37]

Many agree that the alter ego of Miley Stewart is a big draw to viewers. By watching *Hannah Montana*, viewers can live out their own fantasies of what it would be like to be a rock star. "Ah! If we could all live the life of Hannah Montana, pop star by night (and a little of the day) and normal, regular girl-kid the rest of the time," writes Marilyn Moss, TV and movie reviewer. "We'd have the best of both worlds: one that holds great celebrity and fame and a second that gives us that regular kind of life with family and friends."[38]

Mixed Reviews

After the first shows of *Hannah Montana* ran, critics gave their opinions of the show. Some critics consider it well written and acted. Moss writes:

In this best-of-both-worlds kind of universe that the folks at Disney make so appealing, everything works out, and in 22 minutes, give or take, every week. Series creators Michael Poryes, Rich Correll and Barry O'Brien make sure of that. The entire production also is star-kissed with color, good humor and fantastical fantasies that every tween girl can hook in to.[39]

However, not all critics agree with this opinion. "*Hannah Montana* may be a brilliantly marketed show, but it isn't a very good sitcom,"[40] writes Jaime Weinman, a TV show reviewer. He felt that the performers overacted and the subplots were unfunny. Viewers, however, did not seem to notice or care about any negative reviews. During its first season, *Hannah Montana* exploded into a hit show, and its stars became famous.

Miley the Singer

Miley's fame continued to build as Disney launched her singing career. In June 2006 Miley Cyrus made her debut performing as Hannah Montana at a concert at Disney World. On October 24, 2006, Walt

Luxury Vehicle

As one of the richest teenagers in the world, Miley can afford to buy a luxury car. There is one problem. She is not old enough to drive. However, Miley has found another luxury to indulge in—bikes. She is a bike collector. Electra bikes are her favorite. "I like their old-school design, and they're fun to ride," she says. She tries to go on a four-mile ride every day when she is at home. Miley plans to keep collecting bikes. However, another vehicle may be in her future. When she is old enough to drive, she already knows what kind of car she wants. "I want a vintage Corvette," she told Jay Leno.

Quoted in *People*, "Hollywood's Richest Kids," May 5, 2008, p. 97.

Disney Records released Miley Cyrus's first album, *Hannah Montana: Songs from and Inspired by the Hit Series.*

On the soundtrack Miley sings songs that she performs as Hannah Montana on the show. Additionally the soundtrack includes four songs by other artists. The last track on the album, "I Learned from You," is sung by Miley and her father as themselves. The album was a major successs. It debuted at number one on the U.S. Billboard 200 and remained at the top for two weeks. The album was the first TV soundtrack to debut on the chart at number one.

Eight singles from the album, including the theme song "The Best of Both Worlds," charted on the Billboard Hot 100. The soundtrack was the eighth best-selling album of 2006

Musicians Miley and Billy Ray Cyrus perform at the 2008 CMT Music Awards in Nashville, Tennessee, in April 2008.

in the United States. It sold nearly 2 million copies its first year. By 2008 the soundtrack had sold 3.2 million copies in the United States and over 4 million copies worldwide.

In addition to Miley being Hannah Montana on the soundtrack, Disney saw her potential as her own singer. They offered, and Miley accepted, a four-album record deal with Hollywood Records, part of the Disney Group, for her own albums. "I've always loved singing, and I've always loved acting and dancing," says Miley. "Getting this opportunity with Disney, I get to do it all. They let you do everything you love."[41]

Pop Star on Tour

As more and more people listened to the soundtrack, Miley became a pop star. Her talent was a part of this success, but Disney's formula to make its sitcom stars into pop stars was also a major factor. "What made Hannah/Miley a phenom was Disney's learning to use its vast, multimedia holdings," explains James Poniewozik, *Time* magazine writer. "Its stars—young, eager and grateful for the exposure—debut on the Disney Channel. They record CDs for Disney Music. Their music is played on Radio Disney network."[42]

No matter what the reason, preteens and teenagers were listening to Miley Cyrus, and they wanted to see her in person. This led to Miley's first concert tour. At just thirteen years old, she went on tour as Hannah Montana. Miley opened for the Cheetah Girls, a girl group created by Disney, in the fall of 2006 for the first twenty dates of their tour. Additionally she opened for them at their tour's finale in Reliant Stadium in Houston, Texas. The concert was the most successful concert in the stadium since Elvis Presley last played there. Within three minutes, the concert had already sold eighty thousand tickets. When Miley toured with the Cheetah Girls, girls packed into the arenas and yelled, "Hannah! Hannah!"

Following the tour Miley continued to make live appearances on her own. She sang, as Hannah Montana, in the 2006 Macy's Day Parade in November. She went on to sing at the Walt Disney World Christmas Day Parade on Christmas and on New Year's Eve for the Disney Channel special.

On March 28, 2007, Miley, as Hannah Montana, performed live at the Koko Club in London, England. The concert aired live on the United Kingdom's version of the Disney Channel. The taped version of *Hannah Montana: Live in London* then broadcast in the United States and other countries following the live UK broadcast.

Wearing Your Own Face

As Miley's fame exploded, Disney executives decided to create Hannah Montana merchandise. In December 2006 Disney Consumer Products announced a line of products inspired by the show. The products included Hannah Montana apparel, handbags, and accessories available at Macy's department stores nationwide. When these items sold millions, Disney created new products. These included Hannah Montana stationery, posters, bookmarks, greeting cards, gift wrap, and party goods. This merchandise was sold at nationwide stores such as Wal-Mart and Party City.

The Hannah Montana clothing was popular among young girls. The clothes were for girls who wore sizes 7 to 16. Miley decided to check out some of the Hannah Montana clothes during a visit to Tennessee. "When I was in Nashville, I went to our Macy's and went and tried on all the Hannah Montana stuff," she says. "Then I said 'This is weird, I'm wearing my face.'"[43]

Hannah Montana toys then became popular. In August 2007 Play Along Toys sold Hannah Montana fashion dolls and singing dolls, as well as a Miley Stewart doll. More Hannah dolls were released in November, along with Oliver and Lilly dolls. These dolls became one of the most popular Christmas toys in 2007, beating Barbie and Bratz dolls as the desired toy for young girls.

For Miley it seemed a little unreal that all these products were about her and her character. "It's weird. I was playing the video game and they made my hair like eight sizes too big," she jokes. "I'm like, 'Is that really what you guys think of me? You really think of me with this enormous hair?' It's really crazy to see all the things they have out. It's really weird to see in stores but it's really fun, too."[44]

Hannah Montana toys became popular after the TV show hit it big.

Disney executives see the products as ways that girls can continue to enjoy the *Hannah Montana* show in their own lives. "Disney has found the perfect marketing strategy for Hannah Montana: make girls fall in love with the heroine's two identities, and sell them twice the amount of merchandise by creating toys and hairpieces for both,"[45] writes Jamie Weinman. *People* magazine reported that sales of Hannah Montana merchandise for the 2007–2008 fiscal year would generate $1 billion. Miley Cyrus receives an unpublished percentage of these sales.

Miley's Daily Life

Playing Hannah Montana made Miley rich and famous. Her life changed completely. She went from being a typical middle school student and cheerleader in 2005 to a celebrity superstar in 2006. Her daily life became significantly different than it once was.

A typical day for Miley depends on what time of the year it is. In the beginning of the year, she typically films the *Hannah Montana* series. During this time she lives a somewhat normal teenage

Taxis for Miley

In 2007 Miley got to fly to London to film *Hannah Montana: Live in London*. During her stay she spent much of the time working on the show. However, she was able to get some time to tour the city. Of all the sights, such as the Tower of London, Big Ben, and Buckingham Palace, Miley found the more common sights the most interesting. "I love London. I love all the cool buildings," she says. "The biggest thing—I feel like such a geek—is all the taxis and the way people drive on the opposite [side of the] road are awesome. So, even the little things [Londoners] don't think about I think are totally awesome."

Quoted in BBC, "Hotseat: Hannah Montana," March 28, 2007. http://news.bbc.co.uk/cbbcnews/hi/newsid_6480000/newsid_6484900/6484997.stm.

life. She and her father drive to the same place each day. The difference is that instead of going to school like most teenagers, Miley goes to work. However, Miley compares working on the set with the other actors to going to school with her friends.

When not filming the show, Miley's schedule is more irregular. Depending on the day, she may be recording music, on tour, or doing appearances and interviews. She sometimes is at home, but more often she is on the road. During her tour with the Cheetah Girls, she traveled to a new city every few days. When the tour finished, she flew all over the United States making appearances on various shows.

Immediate Fame

It took Miley time to get used to being an instant celebrity. Miley had grown up around reporters, photographers, and fans. However, the paparazzi and fans were trying to see her father, not her. As she grew up, when news reporters did take Miley's picture, it was only because she was Billy Ray Cyrus's daughter.

After the *Hannah Montana* premiere, Miley became the most famous one of the Cyrus family. People wanted to take her picture, interview her, and get her autograph. The fame both excited Miley and made her nervous. She thought it was fun to be noticed and talked to, but also a bit overwhelming. "Once I went out and people started asking me for my autograph, which was the day after *Hannah Montana* first aired, on March 24, 2006," she says of the fame. "It was insane."[46]

She quickly discovered that this recognition would become a typical part of her day. Whether she went shopping or out to a movie, people came up to her to talk or get a picture. She jokes about how everyone knows about everything she does. "I went to Universal (Studios Hollywood theme park) with my brother and a friend," says Miley. "The recognition was immediate. It was

Miley Cyrus gets ready to autograph a Hannah Montana poster for two young fans.

craziness—all the kids on every ride. I felt like I was going to hurl after one ride and all the kids were like, 'Hannah Montana is about to puke!'"[47]

To Miley the hard part of being recognized is not always being able to enjoy her favorite activities. Miley has always loved shopping. Although she now has more money to spend when shopping, it is not as easy to do so. Miley and her mom used to go to stores and the mall for shopping. As Miley became famous, she found this was difficult. "The last time me and my mom went, it turned out to be not such a good idea," says Miley. "People rushed into the store we were in and they had to shut the doors until everyone would go away. It was crazy."[48]

Miley admits that other activities are also harder. When she and her family go out to dinner they are often approached by fans throughout the meal. When she goes biking, one of her favorite activities, she sometimes is chased by the paparazzi.

Overall, though, Miley feels blessed to be in her position. She says the hard part of fame is worth getting to do what she loves. "There's nothing like being on a set where you are there to make other people happy and to make them laugh," she says. "That's the best job in the world."[49]

Chapter 4

Balancing Act

In some ways, Miley Cyrus's life is similar to that of her Miley Stewart character. Like Miley Stewart, Miley Cyrus needs to balance both her life as a pop star and as a normal teenage girl. Unlike Miley Stewart, Miley Cyrus does not have a secret identity. As a result, her pop star life often affects her "regular" life.

Miley relies on family, friends, and faith to balance the growing pressures of teen stardom with being a normal teen. She still wants to enjoy being a kid even though she is often treated as an adult because she is a celebrity. "Being famous is like a dream come true," she says. "But it's really difficult because you lose your freedom. I don't want to lose being a kid."[50]

Family Rules

Miley's parents play a major role in keeping Miley from getting caught up in the pop star life. They treat her as a regular kid, give her rules, and expect her to follow them. They also provide her advice on how to stay grounded.

Each parent performs a role to keep Miley grounded. Her father acts more as her friend than a parent. He makes sure that Miley knows she can talk to him about anything. Because he works with Miley, Billy Ray Cyrus is on the set with her during filming and can keep tabs on her life. "We're really close," says Miley. "I feel like I can tell my dad anything. When we come home, we forget that we even work together and just hang out."[51] Also, because of his own fame, Miley's father gives her lessons on how to handle being a celebrity.

Miley Cyrus and her mom, Tish Cyrus. Miley's mom makes sure Miley follows family rules and keeps up with her schoolwork.

Miley's mother, Tish Cyrus, is the disciplinarian. She makes the rules and enforces them. Tish says she makes a lot of rules to keep Miley in check. For example, she enforces Miley's midnight bedtime on concert nights. On tour, Tish also ensures that Miley is up in the morning to study for three hours with a tutor, which she must do to fulfill her school requirements. Tish says, "Most everybody in her life is 'yes, yes, yes. You're great.' I'm the one to say, 'You can't do this.' I do it because I love her."[52]

Miley's parents also make sure they are with her and her brothers and sisters much of the time. A lot of celebrities Miley's age are seen out at parties and traveling on their own—not Miley. François Navarre, the proprietor of the X17 photo agency, the leader in candid celebrity shots, says:

> Her mom is constantly with her. Which is different from ['High School Musical' stars] Vanessa Hudgens and Ashley Tisdale. They're always without their moms, whereas Miley is always with hers. Miley's really monitored, really watched and controlled by her parents, whereas the other girls are driving their Porsches and going to stores by themselves.[53]

No Place Like Home

Although Miley's parents spend much time with her, they realize that as a teenager she needs her own space. Miley has her own area, including a bedroom and living area, in their Los Angeles house. Miley loves hanging out in her rooms and having friends over.

What she likes most about her area of the house is that she decorated it herself. Miley says:

> The walls are this cool blue, and they've got big circles in metallic on it, and they have the words "vogue" and "chic" everywhere. And I've got candles because I'm really into yoga and stuff like that. So I have that, and all my lights. I have little plants and flowers everywhere. It's really relaxing. And then I've got these big zebra chairs. They're so cool! My bedroom is modeled after this swanky hotel.[54]

Miley Cyrus at a fund-raiser for the American Society for the Protection of Animals (with Davinci the dog and Anne Marie Lucas). Miley loves animals.

Miley also likes being at home because she has fun with her brothers and sisters. They do a lot of activities together, like choreographing dances and putting on their own concerts. Her brother Braison says that Miley will have them all do karaoke together. He and their sister Noah join in for the dances. "They get in her room in front of the I-chat . . . and videotape themselves dancing,"[55] Tish says of Miley and her siblings. For fun, Miley and her brothers and sisters also throw pool parties and cookouts, although Miley admits they do not actually cook the food. They get take out and eat it by the pool.

Another part of home that Miley loves is her animals. In addition to keeping many animals at their Nashville home, Miley also has several in Los Angeles. Most are rescued. "My dog Fluke is a golden retriever mix. We found her in a box on the side of the street. She is a lucky dog. Her mom was a lab/beagle, and so she has these huge ears. She's just the cutest thing in the world. She's a good dog," Miley says. "And my big German shepherd, he had been like kicked around and really treated badly, so we took him in."[56] The animals often are in her room. At times she will have five dogs and a couple of cats keeping her company.

Fitting in School

Outside of her home, Miley also continues to do what other teenagers her age do—go to school. However, her school life is different from most kids'. She attends Options for Youth, a flexible school that allows kids like Miley, who have changing schedules, still to meet school requirements.

At Options for Youth she has a teacher who assigns Miley work that she can do at home. Her meetings with her teacher are scheduled to fit in between her filming times. However, Miley's teacher is not easy on her just because her school is more flexible than most. He tells Miley that everyone is watching him because of her so he makes sure she has plenty of homework.

Miley says the hard part about school is trying to accomplish all her schoolwork while still working as an actor and singer full-time. She may work for forty-five minutes acting, then do an hour of school, then go back to acting for another forty-five minutes.

Sister Contest

Miley knew that being famous meant that people would want to meet her and get to know her. However, she never expected her own sister to be one of these people. A few weeks after the first *Hannah Montana* episode aired, Miley's six-year-old sister, Noah, confessed something to Miley. Noah admitted that she had entered a contest on the Disney Channel Web site. When Miley asked what the contest was for, Noah replied that it was to win backstage passes to a concert featuring the network's newest star—Miley. "You live with me!" Miley responded. Then she jokingly warned Noah not to swipe anything from her bedroom to sell on eBay.

Quoted in Jacque Steinbery, "Hannah Montana: A Tale of Two Tweens," *New York Times*, April 20, 2006. www.nytimes.com/2006/04/20/arts/TV/20cyru.html?ei=5088&en= ce83bf6f2ce0ed7d&ex=1303185600.

Like most kids, she has certain subjects she likes and dislikes. "Language is my favorite. Math, I really do not like. I'm pretty good at it but I just can't focus on it for my life," says Miley. "I don't like numbers. I've decided that. This year I don't like numbers."[57]

Down Time

Although Miley is busy between school and work, she still finds time to relax and have fun. One of her favorite hobbies is writing. In addition to writing songs, Miley loves to write stories. She wrote a book titled *The Diary of Priscilla's Coffeehouse* about people she had met at a coffee shop. She does not intend to publish it and wants to keep it as a book for herself.

Miley also likes to exercise in her free time. In 2007 she hired Harley Pasternak to be her personal fitness trainer. Pasternak is known for working with stars such as Jessica Simpson and Mandy Moore. Miley has said that she has a lot of energy, which is why

Miley Cyrus and friend and fellow entertainer Nick Jonas enjoy the Viper ride at Six Flags Magic Mountain.

she enjoys working out. She also likes to try different ways to stay in shape and recently got into yoga.

Miley also relaxes by hanging out with her friends. Some of their activities include playing video games, dancing, and singing. She and her friends go out on dates, but typically in group situations, according to her father. *People* magazine ran an article with a rumor that she dated Nick Jonas from the Jonas Brothers, a popular all-boy pop group. However, Miley and Nick have admitted that they were only good friends.

Faith First

With everything going on in her life, Miley turns to faith to keep centered. She believes everything she does in life is part of God's plan for her. "Faith is a big part of my life," Miley says. "I recently read a book titled *Girl Talk with God* about a teen girl's conversations with God, and I feel that I'm here in Hollywood because of faith and God's will."[58]

The Cyrus family actively keeps faith a part of their lives. Just as they did in Tennessee, Miley and her family regularly attend church in California. Miley is seen and often photographed by reporters heading into or out of Montrose Church in a suburb of Los Angeles.

Miley believes that her faith makes her more responsible and less caught up in excessive partying like other young stars such as Lindsay Lohan and Britney Spears. "I think it's my faith that keeps me grounded, especially because I'm a Christ follower for sure," Cyrus explains. "Live like Christ and he'll live in you, and that's what I want to do."[59]

Dealing with the Spotlight

Miley's faith and family values help her deal with all the pressures of being a celebrity. One of the pressures is that she is a role model to millions of kids. To Miley this means that she must try always to act in way that positively affects these kids. She strives to achieve a hip, but still wholesome, image.

Being a role model affects Miley's daily decisions. These decisions include deciding what to wear. A stylist helps her choose

Although a stylist helps Miley choose her clothing, Miley is a typical teen and provides a lot of input about her likes and dislikes.

her clothes, but Miley gives the stylist input. "I say what I'm comfortable in and what I like and nothing that's too out there," Miley explains. "I like to look kind of like what girls would want to look up to, and their moms and dads will say, 'Hey, that's cool. That's different.'"[60]

Although Miley enjoys being a role model, she does not always enjoy the constant scrutiny she gets as a celebrity. Every place she goes, whether it is to a coffee shop or even church, she is almost always followed by several members of the paparazzi. They take nonstop pictures. "Just having a camera on you all the time gets kind of frustrating," Miley says. "If you make mistakes, the whole world knows about it. It's not just your family or friends. If you say something really dumb or do something really stupid, the whole world knows about it. My friends will call me, 'did you see that commercial? You are such a nerd'. I'm like 'thanks, guys.'"[61]

Miley's father has issues with the paparazzi always approaching Miley. He feels they cross the line when they stalk her everywhere she goes. He has confronted them in the past, reminding them that she is just a girl. "The problem with the paparazzi is they literally and figuratively take away your ability to be off camera," says Blair Berk, a defense lawyer for celebrities. "You're never offstage. When you're walking down a sidewalk and there are 50 cameras, it's an entirely artificial existence. It seems to me, particularly with teenagers, there's already so much self-consciousness."[62]

Negative Press

Another pressure of being a celebrity is dealing with rumors. Miley learned this early on. It was September 24, 2007. The day did

Being Hannah

Although Miley likes playing Hannah Montana, it is not always easy. Transforming into Hannah Montana takes work. "To be Hannah is crazy. It's a lot harder than to be me," Miley says. "It takes a lot of work, which I couldn't do all the time. It obviously includes a wig, which is hard because you have to take all of this mop and put it underneath this wig. Then there's lots of glitter and lots of cool clothes. It definitely takes some extra hard work to get ready." Once she is transformed, Miley does not always find it easy being Hannah Montana. The main problem is the wig. Miley says it is heavy, hot, and itchy.

Quoted in *The Oprah Winfrey Show*, "Q & A with Miley Cyrus," December 20, 2007. www.oprah.com/tows/slide/200712/20071220/slide_20071220_350_105.jhtml.

Although Miley Cyrus is grateful for her success, she realizes that one major disadvantage of being a celebrity is not having as much private time as she would like.

not start off well for Miley. She woke up and remembered she had to get fitted for braces. That turned out to be the least of her problems. Miley soon found out that a false rumor about her had started on the Internet.

The rumor was that Miley, only fourteen, was pregnant. The paparazzi stood outside the Cyrus's Toluca Lake, California, home all day waiting for a glimpse of her so they could ask her if it was true. She could not ride her bike, which she usually does each day with her brother Braison. Miley ended up crying. Her father comforted her. He sat and talked with her. Billy Ray told Miley, "You know what the funny thing is? In two hours, it's forgotten—like that. Tomorrow there's going to be something bigger and better than this stupid thing."[63]

Another bad day occurred when less-than-wholesome photos of Miley appeared on the Internet. Unfortunately for Miley these pictures were real and not a rumor. In April 2008 people saw photos of Miley showing her midriff while lying across a boy's lap, whom some speculated was her boyfriend. Other photos showed her wearing a white tank top and deliberately revealing a green bra. Many parents of *Hannah Montana* fans were upset because they thought the photos were too revealing for a fifteen-year-old.

Just a teenager, Miley has had to learn to deal with rumors and criticism for certain actions. However, she realizes this is a part of being a celebrity. Miley says she focuses on her fans and their support as she deals with negative press.

Handling Money

In addition to finding ways to deal with fame, Miley also has had to learn how to deal with her wealth. She makes millions each year from her singing, acting, tours, and merchandise. Some sources estimate she will become a billionaire before she is eighteen years old.

Miley's parents play a major role in overseeing her money. They want to make sure she does not become overly spoiled. Although Miley's mother and father allow her to spend money on some expensive items, such as clothes, they limit how much she gets. "A lot of it goes into her [investment fund] which she can't get until she's 18. At the end of the day, she doesn't have much left,"[64] explains her mother. They give her an allowance and she has a credit card, but her mother takes the card away if she finds Miley spending too much.

Miley's parents also encourage her to give her money to worthy causes. Miley chooses to donate a lot of money to help others. According to *OK!* magazine she donates one thousand dollars a week to her church. Additionally Miley has supported charities such as American Red Cross and the Libby Ross Foundation, which helps fight breast cancer.

Miley's Music

Miley not only has to balance being rich and famous with being a typical teenager, she also has to balance her singing life. She sings as both Hannah Montana and herself.

In 2006 fans only heard Miley sing Hannah Montana songs. She sang as Hannah Montana on the show, recorded Hannah Montana songs, and toured as Hannah Montana. As much as Miley liked the Hannah Montana music, after the first year she wanted people to hear her own music.

Miley composes and writes lyrics on her own. Her own songs are different from Hannah Montana songs. "Hannah is more peppy pop," says Miley. "Miley is more edgy, but still girlie."[65] Miley's musical taste has been influenced by a wide range of musicians. Her favorites include the Wreckers and the Killers. She also likes her father's music, Willie Nelson, and Dolly Parton, but is emphatic that she does not want to be a country singer.

Miley says she gets ideas for the songs from her experiences with her family. Often she stays up late and plays her guitar while creating new songs. "I like to play guitar, sing and write music," Miley says when asked what she does for fun. "So practically the same thing that I do when I'm working."[66]

Miley Cyrus appears at the City of Hope hospital benefit concert at the Gibson Amphitheater on September 14, 2008, in Universal City, California. Miley supports multiple charities and donates generously to her church each week.

Breaking Out

Miley's own songs hit the airways in June 2007. Hollywood Records released a double album, *Hannah Montana 2: Meet Miley Cyrus*, on June 26, 2007, eight months after the release of the first soundtrack. The first disc on the double album served as the second *Hannah Montana* soundtrack. The second disc was Miley's debut album as herself. Of the ten songs on the second disc, Miley cowrote eight of them.

The double album was an immediate success. During its first week of sales, it debuted at number one on the U.S. Billboard 200 and sold 326,000 copies. The album remained in the top five for over ten weeks. By 2008 the album had sold more than 3.8 million copies worldwide.

The albums received favorable reviews. Critics noted that on Miley's own tracks, including "Right Here" and "Clear," "this queen of teen sounds like she doesn't need a TV show behind her to shine,"[67] writes Seth Kaufman, music reviewer with Barnes and Noble.

Special Song

All of the songs Miley Cyrus wrote for her album were inspired by her life and are special to her. However, the most meaningful songs that she wrote is "I Miss You." Miley wrote that song about her grandfather, Ron Cyrus, after he died on February 28, 2006.

She first performed the song in the *Hannah Montana* episode "She's a Super Sneak" as her character Miley Stewart. Miley's character sang the chorus of the song as a remembrance for the character's deceased mother.

In December 2007 Miley performed the song on the *Oprah Winfrey Show*. Her father was also on the show. He watched her perform "I Miss You." "It was a very surreal moment sitting here," he says. "And to think that we're sitting here watching little Miley sing that song for my dad is a special moment in my life."[68]

"I Miss You" and the other songs on her double album allowed Miley to come out of her Hannah Montana character. Miley's fans responded with great enthusiasm. Their response encouraged her to try more projects on her own. Although she still enjoyed being Hannah Montana, Miley decided that it was time to let her fans see more of Miley.

Chapter 5

More than Montana

Miley wants the world to hear her own voice. It did after the *Hannah Montana 2: Meet Miley Cyrus* album was released. With the album's success, Miley became known for her own music. Millions of fans listened to, danced to, and sang along with songs cowritten and performed by Miley. The popularity of her album led to the first concert tour where Miley performed many songs as herself.

The *Best of Both Worlds* tour of North America began on October 18, 2007, in St. Louis, Missouri. The initial plan called for fifty-five dates. The tickets were available for sixty-three dollars. One dollar of each ticket went to the City of Hope Foundation, which helps fight cancer.

Soaring Prices

These tour dates sold out within minutes. As soon as tickets were available, ticket brokers went online and bought most of them. Many fans did not have a chance to buy tickets online. Instead they had to buy them from the brokers. Fans discovered that the brokers were selling them from $350 to $2,000 apiece.

Five states—Michigan, North Carolina, Kentucky, Massachusetts, and Rhode Island—limit brokering. For example, in Rhode Island, brokers can only increase ticket prices from the original cost by three dollars, or 10 percent above face value, whichever is greater. However, other states allow the brokers to charge whatever they feel like charging.

Several fans' parents were upset at the high prices. Miley, her family, and Disney felt bad for the fans but could not do anything about the brokers. "It's really unfortunate, and there is nothing we can do to stop it. These inflated costs only benefit the brokers. We were very pleased to hear that various law enforcement agencies are beginning to look into these practices,"[69] a Disney representative said.

Miley and Disney did extend the tour to give more fans a chance to see it. Fourteen additional shows were added to the tour. The tour ended up running for sixty-nine dates until January 31, 2008.

The Concerts

The concerts were planned carefully. The opening act appeared first. For most of the tour, the Jonas Brothers were the opening act. After the Jonas Brothers performed, Miley entered the stage as Hannah Montana.

For half of the show, Miley sang and danced as Hannah Montana. Then Miley went backstage and changed out of her Hannah Montana clothes, wig, and makeup and put on her own clothes. For the second half of the concert, she played and sang songs as herself. "This tour was a really good way of [creating my own identity outside of Hannah Montana]," says Miley. "Just kind of breaking out and having my music. . . . You get to go out in front of 20,000 people every night and show who you really are."[70]

Miley worked hard during each concert. She sang and danced eighteen songs over ninety minutes. In between songs she rushed backstage for seven outfit changes. Her outfits were complex with a mix of glitter, black boots, tennis shoes, miniskirts, corsets, and tank tops. During her songs as Hannah Montana, she wore her blond wig and extra makeup.

Successful Shows

Although there was some negative press regarding ticket prices, the tour was a major success. In 2007 ticket sales from the tour brought in $36 million. This tour was one of the year's top twenty–grossing concert tours in North America.

Miley Cyrus performs during her Best of Both Worlds tour in Philadelphia in December 2007.

Fans of Miley Cyrus and Hannah Montana are very devoted to their favorite performer.

Additionally the reviews of the concerts were positive. Alison Bonagura of Country Music Television writes:

Happy, little girl-power songs like "Life's What You Make It" and "Nobody's Perfect" were just the kind of songs the under-15 crowd wanted to hear and scream along with. And while she looked a little edgier after she lost the Hannah Montana wig and came out onstage as herself, the songs were all basically the same, but in a good way, though. Every single [song] has a positive message, without the slightest hint of teen angst or moodiness. Plenty had high-school themes and a handful had just-us-girls themes, like "Girls' Night Out" and "We Can."[71]

The fans also gave the concerts good reviews. At every show, fans screamed and sang along with Miley. Miley appreciated the fans and did what she could to make each show special. "The hardest thing [about touring], I think, is trying to spice up the show each night and keep things fresh," Miley says. "So, I just try to keep it fun. I play around with the dancers and with the band. I try to make the show's focus more about the relationship between everyone onstage, and not just about me."[72]

Life on Tour

As much as Miley loved doing the tour, all of the traveling and work did get tiring. She missed home. To help, many of her family members came on tour with her. Miley's Uncle Mick accompanied the tour as the tour manager. Her mother, grandmother Loretta Finley, and her sisters, Brandi and Noah, traveled with her for most of the tour. Her father, Billy Ray, could not come on the tour because he was on his own concert tour.

While on tour, Tish's mom ensured that Miley kept up with her three hours of schoolwork a day. Between the concerts and school, Miley did get some time to hang out. She, her family friends, and tour mates, such as the Jonas Brothers, played a lot of video games. Their favorite was *Guitar Hero*. "It's your best friends all hanging out together," says Kevin Jonas of the tour. "It's awesome."[73]

Miley's family and friends also made sure she celebrated her birthday while on tour. Her mother arranged a 1980s-themed surprise birthday party on November 21, 2007, two days before Miley's actual birthday. When Miley arrived in her hometown of Franklin, Tennessee, they went to the Factory, a popular place for bands to perform. She thought she was going to see one of her

favorite bands, Paramore, perform. When she went inside, her family and friends from Tennessee were there to surprise her.

She was most excited to see her dad, whom she missed. She raced over to give him a big hug. "I look forward to when I go back to [taping] *Hannah Montana* because what I really miss is

The Jonas Brothers—Nick, Joe, and Kevin—toured with Miley on her Best of Both Worlds tour.

being with him 24/7," says Miley. However, she still stays in touch with him using iChat and iVideo. "My dad sings to me over video chat, which is so cute."[74]

Billy Ray's surprise birthday present for Miley was that he was staying in town to join her onstage at her birthday concert. On her birthday at her concert, Miley and her dad sang their duet "Ready, Set, Don't Go" from his album for her concert encore. There were other birthday surprises at the concert. The Jonas Brothers presented her with fifteen roses at the end of the performance.

Miley in 3-D

The tour's success led to a 3-D concert movie. "Because ticket sales for the tour were so crazy. But also, we didn't want people to see only what happens onstage," Miley explained when asked why they made a movie. "The film goes behind the scenes, so people see the hard work that goes into [doing a tour]. They get to see it in the making."[75]

Body Double

A video posted on YouTube instigated a controversy about Miley's *Best of Both Worlds* tour. The video showed Miley onstage as Hannah. She is dancing with a group of dancers and the Jonas Brothers. During the song, she is taken offstage through a trap door. Immediately after she leaves, another girl dressed like the character Hannah comes on the stage and dances around. The girl motions like she is singing. After the video was posted, representatives for Miley admitted that the girl was a body double. They said the double was used only to transition the show. Miley says that the double did not sing or dance. "It wasn't because I didn't want to sing or because I didn't want to dance . . . it was because of time," explains Miley. "I usually have an hour and a half to go from Hannah to Miley and I was doing this in one minute 50 seconds. So I needed at least three minutes to go and at least get a little drink of water and like chill for a second."

Quoted in Marcela Isaza, "Miley Cyrus Talks About Hannah Montana Craze, Film," *Oakland Tribune*, February 1, 2008. http://findarticles.com/p/articles/mi_qn4176/is_2008 0201/ai_n21227710.

The tour was recorded and released to theaters in Disney Digital 3-D. Filmgoers watched the movie wearing 3-D glasses. This gave them them the feeling that they were at a real concert. The movie shows Miley Cyrus performing as Hannah Montana at her performance in Salt Lake City, Utah. Additionally, the film shows behind-the-scenes action that includes Miley changing from Hannah Montana to herself.

In February 2008 the film opened in the United States at 683 theaters that were able to show digital 3-D movies. The concert film brought in nearly $8.7 million on its opening day. It grossed over $31 million the first weekend. This made it the highest-grossing opening weekend for a film to be released on fewer than one thousand screens. Initially the film was to run a week, but because of its major popularity Disney extended the showing.

More of Miley

The popularity of the tour and movie gave Miley the confidence to take on more projects as herself. One project is the *Miley and Mandy Show*, which airs on the Internet over YouTube. Miley and her friend Mandy Jiroux, a dancer on Miley's *Best of Both Words* tour, started a YouTube channel where they upload videos of themselves. The videos are posted periodically.

Miley says they started the channel after she and Mandy filmed Mandy teaching Miley some dance moves. When they watched the film, they saw how much fun they had together joking around and being silly. "Once we watched back the video we had made

Mandy Jiroux (left) was a dancer on Miley Cyrus's **Best of Both Worlds** *tour. They are good friends and now have their own show,* **Miley and Mandy Show,** *on YouTube.*

we realized that when we were just being ourselves it was much more entertaining than the dance we had put together!" writes Miley on the Web site. "So, we decided to make a YouTube account and load the video and see what the reaction [was]."[76] Thousands of people viewed the video within a day. By June 2008 their channel itself had over 128,000 subscribers.

In the show Miley and Mandy tell jokes, answer questions from fans, sing, and dance. It is informal and often set in Miley's bedroom. An example of one episode is where the two friends are on hold on the telephone. Mandy is waiting to talk on Ryan Seacrest's morning show. They film themselves primping as they wait to talk to him.

Writing and Singing

Miley also had more formal projects in the works. After her *Best of Both Worlds* tour, she worked on a full-length album. Hollywood Records released it on July 28, 2008. The album was titled *Breakout*, and all songs are Miley Cyrus songs.

The first single, "7 Things," was released to radio stations in March 2008. Miley wrote "7 Things" with Antonina Armato and Tim James. On the track Miley sings about an ex-boyfriend who does not give a sincere apology. "And when you mean it, I'll believe it/If you text it, I'll delete it,"[77] Miley sings.

Miley first performed live songs from the album at the 2008 Disney Channel Games in May. She sang the album's title track, "Breakout," and another song from the album, "Fly on the Wall."

Life Writings

Miley also started on another writing project. She decided to write an autobiography of her life. In April 2008 Disney announced that Miley signed a seven-figure book deal with the Disney Book Group.

The book will focus on Miley's life before she played Hannah Montana. It will include stories about growing up in Tennessee with her family. Miley will also write about how she keeps grounded while being a major star. The book will especially focus on her relationship with her mother, Tish, and other close friends and family. "I am so excited to let fans in on how important my relationship with my family is to me," Miley says. "I hope to motivate mothers and daughters to build lifetimes of memories together, and inspire kids around the world to live their dreams."[78] Never-before-seen photos of family will be included in the book.

The Disney Book Group has announced that the book will be published in the spring of 2009. Disney believes the book is another way to inspire Miley's fans. "Miley is a genuine international sensation and we are delighted to deliver her first book to families around the world," said Jeanne Mosure, senior vice president and global publisher of Disney Book Group. "She is a terrific role model, and we are incredibly proud to give kids everywhere the opportunity to connect with her in an entirely new way."[79]

Still Hannah Montana

Although Miley is involved in many new projects as herself, she still enjoys playing Hannah Montana. In April 2008 Disney announced that they renewed *Hannah Montana* for a third season. In May 2008 Miley started working on an even bigger Hannah Montana project.

Production for *Hannah Montana: The Movie* got underway in May 2008. The movie is an adaptation of the *Hannah Montana* TV series. The movie follows the character Miley Stewart as the soaring popularity of her alter ego, Hannah Montana, threatens to take over Miley's life. In the movie Miley Stewart travels back to her hometown of Crowley Corners, Tennessee, to figure out what is really important in life. In real life Miley Cyrus got to travel back to her home state of Tennessee during the filming. The movie was filmed in both Tennessee and California.

Different musicians have become involved in the movie. In June 2008 country group Rascal Flatts announced that it would appear in *Hannah Montana: The Movie*. In addition to appearing, they will perform in the movie. Also, Bucky Covington, who finished in eighth place on the fifth season of *American Idol*, will play a role in the movie. He will appear as a musician.

Singing with Dad

At special performances, such as Miley's birthday concert while on tour and at the Country Music Television Music Awards, she and her father, Billy Ray, sang "Ready, Set, Don't Go." This is a special song that Billy Ray wrote about the day their family found out Disney had picked up *Hannah Montana*. "We knew as a family that we needed to move to Hollywood," Billy Ray says. He initially stayed behind to finish some tasks as the rest of the family moved. "As they drove off, it was that moment of realizing that I was letting go, you know, that my little girl was growing up and there was a lot of change around the corner. And I walked in the house and leaning against the wall there was my old guitar . . . this song just came to me, and it's about letting go as a parent." Billy Ray initially released the song as a solo, but he rereleased it in 2007 as a duet with Miley. In February 2008 the song rose to the number five spot on the U.S. *Billboard* Hot Country Songs chart.

Quoted in *The Oprah Winfrey Show*, "Q & A with Miley Cyrus," December 20, 2007. www.oprah.com/tows/slide/200712/20071220/slide_20071220_350_118.jhtml.

Awards and Shows

Miley's projects both as Hannah Montana and herself have led to many awards. In 2007 she won the Teen Choice Award for female actress in a comedy series. The following year she received the Best Performance of a Lead Young Actress in a TV series at the Young Artist Awards.

In 2008 Miley won Favorite TV Actress and Favorite Female Singer at the Nickelodeon Kids' Choice Awards. The Kids' Choice Awards show how many fans Miley has. These awards are based on viewer votes. Over 88 million viewers cast votes online for the 2008 Kids' Choice Awards.

In addition to receiving awards, Miley has hosted, presented, and sung at numerous awards shows. In front of an audience of ten thousand, she sang "Girls' Night Out" at the 2008 Kids' Choice Awards. One of her favorite award show performances was the 2008 Country Music Television Music Awards. Miley not only co-hosted the event with her father but also got to perform "Ready, Set, Don't Go" with him.

Miley Cyrus poses with her Choice Summer Artist award at the Teen Choice Awards in August 2007.

Growing Up

The question remains whether Miley will be able to transform herself from a tween superstar into an adult rock star and actress. "Within three to five years, Miley will have to face adulthood. Fans grow up, and their youthful interests quickly dissolve. Her challenge will be overcoming the Hannah Montana stereotype. Miley's fans are not thinking about the fact that she will grow up too," writes Donny Osmond, who was a child star himself. "As she does, she'll want to change her image, and that change will be met with adversity."[80]

Already there has been controversy surrounding what many consider racy pictures taken of Miley for *Vanity Fair*. The most controversial of these images shows Miley apparently topless, with a satin sheet around her chest. Her hair and lipstick are mussed in a sexy manner. In other shots, Miley is draped across her father's lap. Famous photographer Annie Leibovitz took the photos. During the photo shoot, Miley's parents and editors for *Vanity Fair* were present.

Some people believe these pictures were taken to show a more adult Miley in an effort to break her teen image. "It seems to be a strategic career move," says Bonnie Vent, of Genesis Creations. "She's already queen of the tweens, so now they need to make her queen of the teen boys."[81]

Many parents of current fans were upset by the sexy nature of the photos. Since the shoot, Miley has apologized for the photos. "I took part in a photo shoot that was supposed to be 'artistic' and now, seeing the photographs and reading the story, I feel so embarrassed," Miley said in a statement. "I never intended for any of this to happen and I apologize to my fans who I care so deeply about."[82]

After a few weeks, the controversy died down. Whether her fans will continue to support her if she tries to establish a more mature image in the future remains to be seen. In the meantime she continues to be one of the most popular teenage superstars. In June 2008 she made *Forbes* magazine's annual Celebrity 100 ranking of the world's most powerful and best-paid celebrities. Miley shows no signs of slowing down.

Introduction: Miley at Madame Tussauds

1. Quoted in Katie Thomson and Elizabeth Grodd, "Billy Ray Cyrus Helps Daughter Miley with 'Pressures of the World,'" ABC News, September 21, 2007. www.abcnews.go.com/2020/Story?id=3634291&page=2.

2. Quoted in Nick Dent, "Miley's Tween Spirit," *Daily Telegraph*, April 20, 2008. www.news.com.au/dailytelegraph/story/0,,22049,23559882-5006011,00.html.

Chapter 1: Named for Greatness

3. Quoted in Access Hollywood, "Billy Ray Cyrus Talks Miley's Star Power." http://video.accesshollywood.com/player/?id=247698#videoid=246488.

4. Quoted in ABC News, "Choosing Family Over Fame and Fortune," March 1994. http://abcnews.go.com/print?id=132388.

5. Quoted in ABC News, "Choosing Family Over Fame and Fortune."

6. Quoted in CNN, "Glenn Beck: Billy Ray Cyrus Interview," December 5, 2007. http://transcripts.cnn.com/TRANSCRIPTS/0712/05/gb.01.html.

7. Quoted in PBS Kids, "It's My Life: Miley Cyrus." http://pbs kids.org/itsmylife/celebs/interviews/miley.html.

8. Quoted in BBC, "Hotseat: Hannah Montana," March 28, 2007. http://news.bbc.co.uk/cbbcnews/hi/newsid_6480000/newsid_6484900/6484997.stm.

9. Quoted in Audrey Hingley, "Hosanna, Montana!" *Today's Christian*, January/February 2008. www.christianitytoday.com/tc/2008/001/1.19.html.

10. Quoted in Marie Morreale, "Star Spotlight: Miley Cyrus,"

Scholastic News. http://teacher.scholastic.com/scholasticnews/
mtm/starspotlight.asp?sf=miley.

11. Quoted in ABC News, "Oscar Exclusive: Stars Dish with Bar-
    bara Walters," February 22, 2008. http://abcnews.go.com/
    Entertainment/Oscars2008/story?id=4318308&page.

12. Quoted in MSNBC, "Life Imitates Art for Teen Actress Miley
    Cyrus," June 4, 2006. www.msnbc.msn.com/id/12975970/.

13. Quoted in Maria Giordono, "Hannah Montana Reconnects
    with Former Teacher," *Tennesseean*, January 10, 2008.
    http://64.233.167.104/search?q=cache:i6LFIU9wO10J:www.te
    nnessean.com/apps/pbcs.dll/article%3FAID%3D/20080110/C
    OUNTY090101/801100344/0/features01+%22Nancy+Sevier
    %22+miley+cyrus&hl=en&ct=clnk&cd=2&gl=us.

14. Quoted in Tribute, "Miley Cyrus aka Hannah Montana Inter-
    view." www.tribute.ca/features/hannahmontana.

15. Quoted in *People*, "Miley Cyrus." www.people.com/people/
    miley_cyrus/biography.

16. Quoted in *The Barbara Walters Special*, ABC, February 24, 2008.

17. Quoted in Luck Media and Marketing Inc., "Billy Ray Cyrus
    and Wife Tish Surprise Daughter Miley with a Daisy Rock
    Girl Guitar at Fan Club Event During CMA Music Festival,"
    June 13, 2004. www.luckmedia.com/daisyrock/photogallery
    .html.

Chapter 2: Big Break

18. Quoted in Jeanne McDowell, "A Disney Star Is Born," *Time,*
    November 30, 2006. www.time.com/time/printout/0,8816,
    1564394,00.html#.

19. *Back Stage West*, "Hannah Montana," November 25, 2004, p. 20.

20. Quoted in McDowell, "A Disney Star Is Born."

21. Quoted in Ann Oldenburg, "Miley Cyrus Fulfills Her Des-
    tiny," *USA Today*, January 14, 2007. www.usatoday.com/
    life/TV/news/2007-01-10-miley-cyrus_x.htm.

22. Quoted in Dent, "Miley's Tween Spirit."

23. Quoted in Oldenburg, "Miley Cyrus Fulfills Her Destiny."

24. Quoted in Beck, "Billy Ray Cyrus Interview."

25. Quoted in Dent, "Miley's Tween Spirit."

26. Quoted in *Children's Digest*, "Catching Up with 'Hannah Montana,'" May–June 2007, p. 16.

27. Quoted in David Hiltbrand, "Newfound Fame on Disney Shouldn't Faze Miley Cyrus," *Philadelphia Inquirer*, May 17, 2006.

28. Quoted in James Poniewozik, "Hurricane Hannah," *Time*, October 18, 2007. www.time.com/time/magazine/article/0,9171, 1673286,00.html.

29. Quoted in Devin Leonard, "Hannah Montana Inc.," *Fortune*, February 5, 2007.

30. Quoted in *Hannah Montana: Pop Star Profile*, DVD, directed by David Kendall. Buena Vista Home Entertainment, Burbank, CA, 2007.

31. Quoted in *Star Scoop*, "Emily Osment," November 2006. www.thestarscoop.com/2006nov/emily-osment.php.

32. Quoted in *Teen Magazine*, "Miley on Miley," Spring 2008, p. 72.

33. Quoted in Champ Clark, "Her Big Breaky," *People Weekly*, April 17, 2006, p. 117.

34. Quoted in Michael Learmouth, "Disney Wishes on New Tween Star: Mouse Hopes It's Found the Next Hilary Duff," *Variety*, February 20, 2006, p. 18.

Chapter 3: Montana Mania

35. Quoted in Andrew Wallenstein, "'Montana' Draws North of 5 Mil.," *Hollywood Reporter*, March 28, 2006, p. 4.

36. Quoted in *Oakland Tribune*, "The Star of Miley Cyrus—Who Plays Hannah Montana—Shines in Tween Land," October 28, 2007.

37. Quoted in Star Scoop, "Emily Osment."

38. Marilyn Moss, "'Hannah Montana,'" *Hollywood Reporter*, March 24, 2006, p. 17.

39. Moss, "'Hannah Montana,'" p. 17.

40. Jaime J. Weinman, "Everybody Loves Hannah Montana: A Show About a Teen Who Is Secretly a Pop Star Has Turned the Disney Channel into the Most Powerful Producer of Kids' Entertainment," *Macleans*, January 14, 2008, p. 72.

41. Quoted in Oldenburg, "Miley Cyrus Fulfills Her Destiny."

42. Quoted in Poniewozik, "Hurricane Hannah."

43. Quoted in Oldenburg, "Miley Cyrus Fulfills Her Destiny."

44. Quoted in Maya Motavilli and Ed Martin, "Miley Cyrus on Season Two *Hannah Montana*," February, 13, 2007. www .mediavillage.com/jmentr/2007/02/13/jmer-02-13-07.

45. Weinman, "Everybody Loves Hannah Montana," p. 72.

46. Quoted in Tim Stack, Margeaux Watson, Lynette Rice, and Jeff Labrecque, "Prodigies," *Entertainment Weekly*, November 30, 2007, p. 80.

47. Quoted in Hiltbrand, "Newfound Fame on Disney Shouldn't Faze Miley Cyrus."

48. Quoted in MSNBC, "Life Imitates Art for Hannah Montana," June 4, 2006. www.msnbc.msn.com/id/12975970.

49. Quoted in Oldenburg, "Miley Cyrus Fulfills Her Destiny."

Chapter 4: Balancing Act

50. Quoted in Michelle Tan, "How Billy Ray and Miley Stay Grounded," *People*, June 21, 2007. www.people.com/people/article/0,,20043304,00.html.

51. Quoted in *People*, "Miley Cyrus."

52. Quoted in Angela Carson, "Hannah Montana Star Miley Cyrus & Nick Jonas Kiss on Stage, Romance," *National Ledger*,

December 3, 2007. www.nationalledger.com/cgi-bin/artman/exec/view.cgi?archive=20&num=17511.

53. Quoted in Rachel Abramowitz, "Paparazzi Have Their Lenses on Miley Cyrus," *Los Angeles Times*, May 28, 2008. www.latimes.com/entertainment/news/celebrity/la-et-brief28-2008may28,0,2650361.story.

54. Quoted in Kelly White, "Miley Face! GL Gets Some Phone Time with the One, the Only," *Girls' Life*, December 2007, p. 36.

55. *Hannah Montana: Pop Star Profile.*

56. Quoted in White, "Miley Face!" *Girls' Life*, p. 36.

57. Quoted in Lynn Barker, "Miley Cyrus: At Hollywood Highland," *Teen Hollywood*, July 5, 2007. www.teenhollywood.com/printerversion.asp?r=152958.

58. Quoted in Hingley, "Hosanna, Montana."

59. Quoted in Hollie McKay, "Pop Tarts: Miley Cyrus 'Faith Keeps Me Grounded,'" *Fox News*, March 28, 2008. www.foxnews.com/story/0,2933,342610,00.html.

60. Quoted in Tim Nudd, "Miley Cyrus: Being a Role Model Starts with the Clothes," *People*, December 20, 2007. www.people.com/people/article/0,,20167543,00.html?xid=rss-fullcontentcnn.

61. Quoted in Barker, "Miley Cyrus."

62. Quoted in Abramowitz, "Paparazzi Have Their Lenses on Miley Cyrus."

63. Quoted in Hiltbrand, "Newfound Fame on Disney Shouldn't Faze Miley Cyrus."

64. Quoted in Hollyscoop, "Miley Cyrus Almost a Billionare," May 5, 2008. www.hollyscoop.com/miley-cyrus/miley-cyrus-almost-a-billionaire_15849.aspx.

65. Quoted in Dent, "Miley's Tween Spirit."

66. Quoted in *The Oprah Winfrey Show*, "Q & A with Miley Cyrus," December 20, 2007. www.oprah.com/tows/slide/200712/20071220/slide_20071220_350_111.jhtml.

67. Seth Kaufman, Barnes and Noble, "Hannah Montana 2: Meet Miley Cyrus," http://music.barnesandnoble.com/Hannah-Montana-2-Meet-Miley-Cyrus/Hannah-Montana/e/5008710 5464.

68. Quoted in *The Oprah Winfrey Show*, "Q & A with Miley Cyrus."

Chapter 5: More than Montana

69. Quoted in Rich Phillips, "Brokers Snatch Joy from Hannah Montana Fans," *CNN*, October 12, 2007. www.cnn.com/2007/SHOWBIZ/TV/10/12/montana.tickets/index.html.

70. Quoted in Marcela Isaza, "Miley Cyrus Talks About Hannah Montana Craze, Film," *Oakland Tribune*, February 1, 2008. http://findarticles.com/p/articles/mi_qn4176/is_20080201/ai_n21227710.

71. Alison Bonagura, "Miley Cyrus Brings Concert Tour to Chicago," *Country Music Television*, January 15, 2008. www.cmt.com/news/articles/1579682/20080115/cyrus__miley.jhtml.

72. Quoted in Vickie An, "Ten Questions for Miley Cyrus," *Time for Kids*, February 1, 2008. www.timeforkids.com/TFK/kids/news/story/0,28277,1709019,00.html.

73. Quoted in Michelle Tan, "The Life of Miley," *People Weekly*, December 10, 2007, p. 100.

74. Quoted in Tan, "The Life of Miley."

75. Quoted in An, "Ten Questions for Miley Cyrus."

76. Miley Cyrus, "The Miley and Mandy Show," YouTube. www.youtube.com/user/mileymandy.

77. Quoted in Jonathon Cohen, "Miley Cyrus Breaks Out with New Album," *Billboard*, May 20, 2008. www.billboard.com/bb com/news/article_display.jsp?vnu_content_id=1003805755.

78. Quoted in Ulrica Wihlborg, "Miley Cyrus Signs Seven-Figure Book Deal," *People*, April 22, 2008. www.people.com/people/article/0,,20194112,00.html.

79. Quoted in Reuters, "Miley Cyrus Signs International Book

Deal with Disney Book Group," April 22, 2008. www.reuters
.com/article/pressRelease/idUS144150+22-Apr-2008
+BW2008 0422.

80. Quoted in Donny Osmond, "The 2008 Time 100," *Time*.
www.time.com/time/specials/2007/article/0,28804,17337
48_1733752_1734628,00.html.

81. Quoted in Rebecca Winters Keegan, "The Miley Cyrus Pics:
Damage Control," *Time*, April 28, 2008. www.time.com/
time/arts/article/0,8599,1735807,00.html.

82. Quoted in Keegan, "The Miley Cyrus Pics."

November 23, 1992

Destiny Hope "Miley" Cyrus is born to Billy Ray and Leticia Cyrus in Franklin, Tennessee.

2003

Miley appears in *Doc*, the show that her father, Billy Ray Cyrus, stars in, and the movie *Big Fish*.

2005

Miley wins the lead role in the Disney series *Hannah Montana*. Billy Ray lands the role as her father on the show.

2006

Hannah Montana becomes the most-watched cable show for kids aged six to eleven.

March 24, 2006

Hannah Montana debuts on the Disney Channel.

October 24, 2006

Walt Disney Records releases Miley's first album, *Hannah Montana: Songs from and Inspired by the Hit Series*. It debuts at number one on the Billboard Top 200.

June 26, 2007

Hollywood Records releases a double album, *Hannah Montana 2: Meet Miley Cyrus*. On it, Miley Cyrus debuts eight songs that she cowrote.

October 18, 2007

The *Best of Both Worlds* tour of North America begins and runs for sixty-nine dates. Tickets sell out immediately.

February 1, 2008

Hannah Montana and Miley Cyrus: Best of Both Worlds Concert, a 3-D film that chronicles her tour, opens in the United States at 683 theaters. The concert film brings in nearly $8.7 million on its opening day.

April 2008

Sexy pictures of Miley taken by famous photographer Annie Leibovitz are released and spark a controversy.

April 14, 2008

Miley and Billy Ray Cyrus host and perform "Ready, Set, Don't Go" at the 2008 Country Music Television Music Awards.

April 23, 2008

Miley signs a seven-figure book deal with Disney Book Group. The book will focus on how she rose to fame and her relationship with her family.

May 2008

Disney's Hollywood Records announces that it will release *Breakout*, Miley's first full-length album under her own name, on July 22, 2008.

June 12, 2008

Forbes includes Miley on its annual Top 100 Most Powerful Celebrities.

November 21, 2008

The Disney animated movie *Bolt* is released. Miley voices the main character, Penny, in the movie.

April 10, 2009

Hannah Montana: The Movie is set for release.

Periodicals

Ann Oldenburg, "Miley Cyrus Fulfills Her Destiny," *USA Today*, January 14, 2007. www.usatoday.com/life/TV/news/2007-01-10-miley-cyrus_x.htm. This article details how Miley's persistence landed her the Hannah Montana role. It discusses what has happened since *Hannah Montana* first aired and Miley's ongoing projects.

People, "Hollywood's Richest Kids," May 5, 2008. This article discusses how much money Miley has made as a pop star/actress and what she does with this money.

Michelle Tan, "How Billy Ray and Miley Stay Grounded," *People*, June 21, 2007. www.people.com/people/article/0,,200433 04,00.html. This article focuses on Miley's life with her family. Specifically it discusses how her parents keep her life as normal as possible despite the fact she is a major celebrity.

Web Sites

Disney Hannah Montana (http://home.disney.go.com/characters/hannahmontana). This section of Disney's Web site provides information about the *Hannah Montana* show and soundtracks. On the site, viewers can also watch *Hannah Montana* videos.

The Miley and Mandy Show (www.youtube.com/user/mileymandy). This is Miley and Mandy's YouTube channel. On this site are videos from Miley Cyrus and her friend Mandy Jiroux of themselves and friends. These are informal videos they periodically post that include them talking, dancing, and laughing.

Miley Cyrus Official Website (www.mileycyrus.com). This is Miley Cyrus's personal Web site. The site is in a magazine format, and viewers can "flip" pages via the keyboard. On the site, readers can learn where Miley currently is and what is occurring in her life and also see pictures of her.

The Oprah Winfrey Show, "Q & A with Miley Cyrus" (www
.oprah.com/tows/slide/200712/20071220/slide_20071220_350
_119.jhtml). This section of the *Oprah Winfrey Show* Web site
provides questions and answers asked of Miley Cyrus during
her December 2007 appearance on *Oprah*. These questions are
about her singing, what it's like to be a pop star, and her everyday life.

DVD

Hannah Montana: Pop Star Profile, DVD. Directed by David Kendall.
Buena Vista Home Entertainment, Burbank, CA. DVD, 2007.
This DVD includes *Hannah Montana* episodes. Additionally, in
the bonus features there is a live performance by Miley Cyrus
as Hannah Montana and an interview with Miley, her mother,
two sisters, and brother.

About the Author

Leanne Currie-McGhee is the author of several children's books published by Lucent and KidHaven. She resides in Norfolk, Virginia, with her husband, Keith, and daughter, Grace.